@RosenTeenTalk

THE IMPORTANCE OF SLEEP

Greg Roza

ROSEN PUBLISHING

Published in 2026 by The Rosen Publishing Group, Inc.
2544 Clinton Street, Buffalo, NY 14224

First Edition

Editor: Greg Roza
Designer: Michael Flynn

Photo Credits: Cover, pp. 1, 5, 45 New Africa/Shutterstock.com; cover (emoji) Cosmic_Design/Shutterstock.com; cover, p. 1 (phone) Vitya_M/Shutterstock.com; pp. 3, 13 Andrey_Popov /Shutterstock.com; pp. 3, 21 Jestercine/Shutterstock.com; pp. 3 , 31 Studio Romantic /Shutterstock.com; pp. 3, 39 F01 PHOTO/Shutterstock.com; p. 7 (top) Motortion Films /Shutterstock.com; p. 7 (bottom) N ON NE ON/Shutterstock.com; p. 9 Monkey Business Images/Shutterstock.com; p. 10 Elena Kalinicheva/Shutterstock.com; p. 11 Antonio Guillem/Shutterstock.com; p. 14 kanyanat wongsa/Shutterstock.com; p. 15 Prostock-studio/Shutterstock.com; p. 16 Melnikov Dmitriy/Shutterstock.com; p. 17 Rumka vodki/Shutterstock.com; p. 19 Ground Picture/Shutterstock.com; p. 22 kimdaman/Shutterstock.com; pp. 23, 26 Andrey_Popov/Shutterstock.com; p. 25 Lysenko Andrii/Shutterstock.com; p. 27 Dragana Gordic/Shutterstock.com; p. 28 Golden Sikorka/Shutterstock.com; p. 29 MAYA LAB/Shutterstock.com; p. 32 Pisit Rapitpunt/Shutterstock.com; p. 33 galka3250/Shutterstock.com; p. 35 Image Point Fr/Shutterstock.com; p. 37 Kittyfly/Shutterstock.com; p. 40 Jacek Chabraszewski/Shutterstock.com; p. 43 vk_st/Shutterstock.com.

Cataloging-in-Publication Data

Names: Roza, Greg.
Title: The importance of sleep / Greg Roza.
Description: Buffalo, NY : Rosen Publishing, 2026. | Series: @RosenTeenTalk | Includes glossary and index.
Identifiers: ISBN 9781725342484 (pbk.) | ISBN 9781725342491 (library bound) | ISBN 9781725342507 (ebook)
Subjects: LCSH: Sleep--Physiological aspects. | Sleep.
Classification: LCC QP425.R69 2026 | DDC 612.821083--dc23

Manufactured in the United States of America

CPSIA Compliance Information: Batch #CWRYA26. For Further Information contact Rosen Publishing at 1-800-237-9932.

CONTENTS

Chapter 1

We All Need Sleep

Tia gasped as her head hit her desk. She blinked and rubbed her forehead. The kids around her laughed. She rubbed her eyes and glanced around the room. The whiteboard was filled with numbers and diagrams; they didn't make any sense to her. The classroom clock said 10:43 … two minutes until the bell rang. *I slept through math again!*

Mr. Robelard asked to have a word with her. He was worried about her, since this wasn't the first time she had fallen asleep during his class. Her grades were poor recently, and she never seemed prepared for tests. Mr. Robelard was worried that Tia might be having trouble at home. She promised to do better.

Tia left the room yawning. *Why can't I sleep at night?* she wondered as she hurried to PE.

Do you get a good night's sleep every night? Do you feel tired in school?

CATCHING Zs

Sleep is a natural process that almost all animals experience. Some animals sleep a lot. Koalas can sleep up to 22 hours a day! Male lions may sleep up to 20 hours a day. On the other hand, African elephants may only sleep two hours a day.

A baby human usually sleeps up to 16 hours day. They get tired from all the growing and learning they're doing! Adults need about eight hours of sleep. Teens need up to 10 hours of sleep. However, many teens don't get enough sleep, and it can affect their health and lifestyle.

Some teens are tired because they stay up late at night. Others are tired because they spend too much time looking at their phone. These are things they can change. For other teens, however, tiredness and a lack of sleep might be signs of an illness or **disorder**.

How many hours of sleep do you usually get each night?

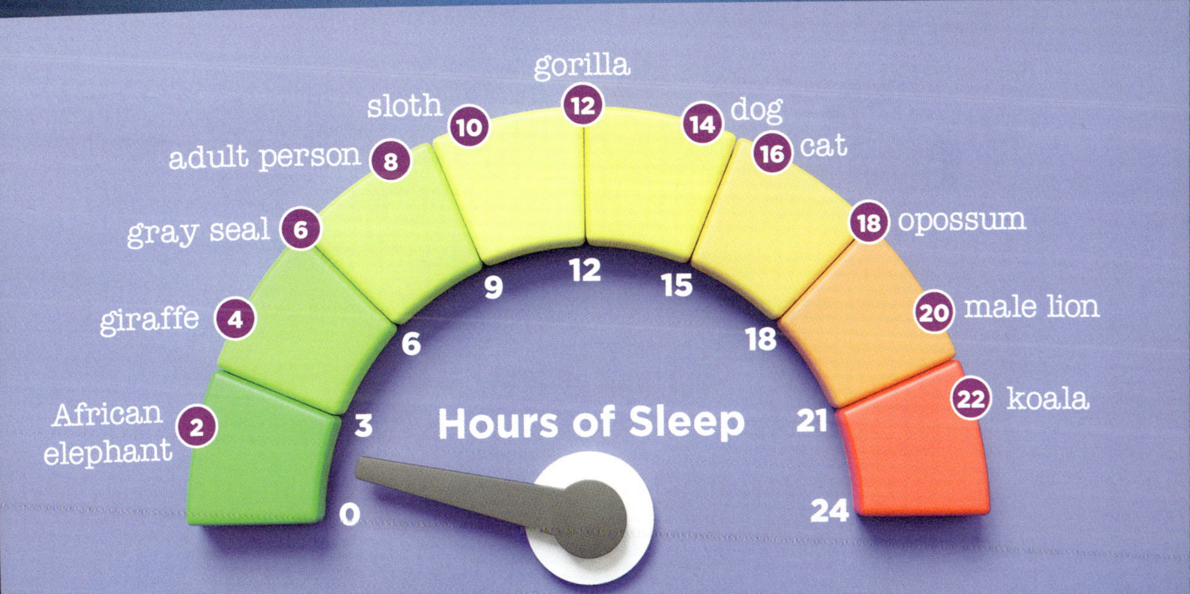

SLEEP DEPRIVATION

Lack of sleep, also called sleep deprivation, is caused by many things. A barking dog or a beeping car horn can cause it. However, so can bad feelings caused by a family fight. **Depression** and **anxiety** can result in sleeplessness.

Sleep gives the body time to rest, grow, and heal. This helps the body fight illnesses. Sleep also builds up energy for the coming day. When we don't get enough sleep, we feel tired and we lack energy needed to get through a typical day. We also get sick more often.

The brain also needs regular sleep to work properly. If you've ever stayed up late and got up early the next morning, you likely know how sleep depravation feels. You feel tired, but you also have a "foggy brain." This means that it's hard to **concentrate** on things like school work.

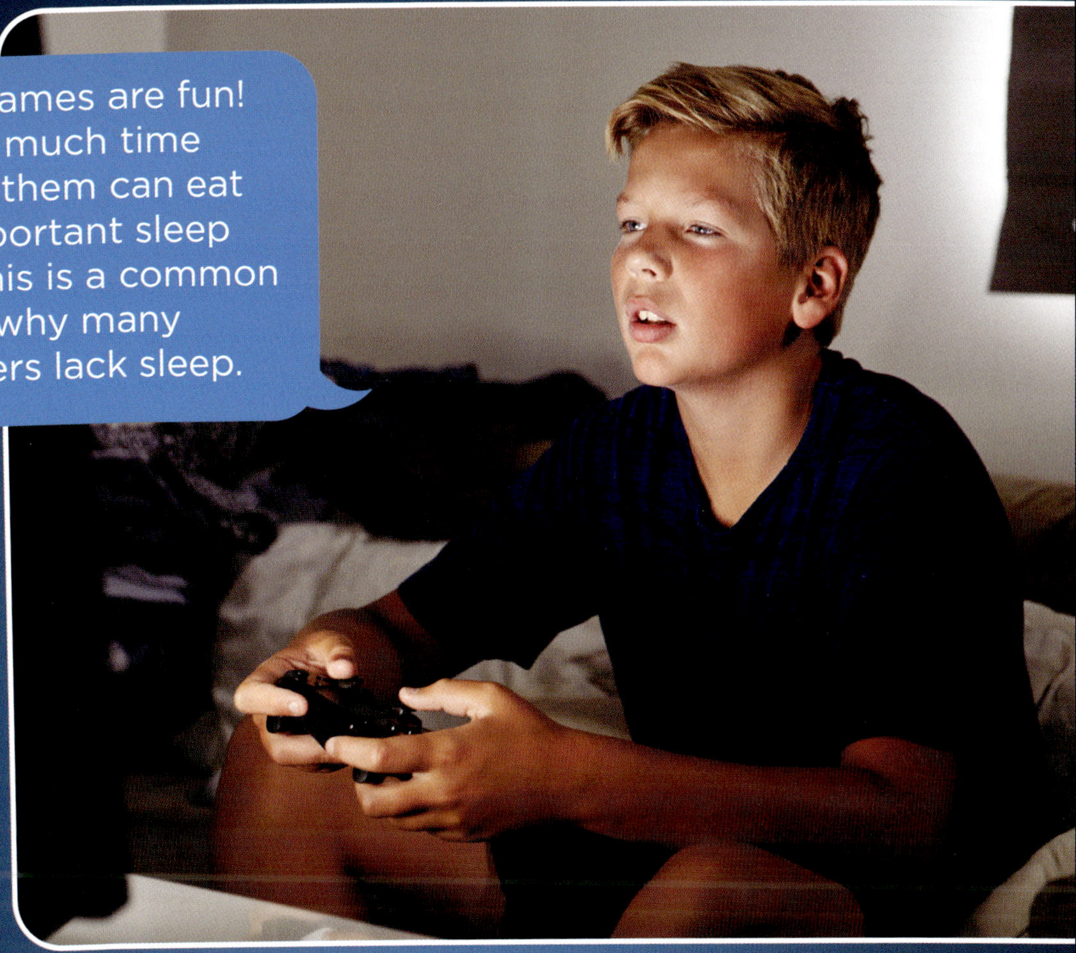

Video games are fun! But too much time playing them can eat into important sleep time. This is a common reason why many teenagers lack sleep.

CAUSES OF SLEEPLESSNESS

- caffeinated drinks (soda, coffee, tea)
- poor sleep **schedule**
- illnesses and **allergies**
- physical problems or pain
- snoring
- depression and anxiety
- **stress**
- noises

TIME TO ACT

Now, imagine if sleeplessness happened to you several times a week or even every night. Imagine if you felt like there's nothing you can do about it. This is a reality for many people. For these people, the cause of sleeplessness could be something more serious than staying up late. An inability to get to sleep regularly is called insomnia.

Some illnesses can result in a lack of sleep. This might be due to pain. Sometimes it's hard to even say why someone can't sleep. At that point, it's time to see a doctor.

You can read more about how sleep affects a teen's life here: **www.sleepfoundation.org/teens-and-sleep**

Getting less than seven to eight hours of sleep a night is called sleep deficit. Deficit means lower than what was expected or needed. Don't suffer in silence—tell an adult you trust about your sleep problems.

Chapter 2

SLEEP SCIENCE

Sleep is part of our bodies' natural circadian rhythms. Circadian rhythms are the patterns our bodies follow during a 24-hour period. They're like "internal clocks" that affect when we wake up or go to sleep, when we eat, and how hot or cold our bodies are. Some rhythms are **automatic** and we may not know they're happening inside us. For example, your stomach makes certain **chemicals** when you're preparing to eat. These chemicals help break down food.

Circadian rhythms are linked to the human sleep cycle. When we don't get regular sleep at night, our internal clocks can get mixed up. This leads to drowsiness, lack of focus, and clumsiness.

Word Origin

The term "circadian" comes from the Latin words *circa* ("about") and *diem* ("day'). So, circadian means "about a day."

Many people work the third shift, or the overnight shift. They must retrain their circadian rhythms to be awake and active when most of us are asleep and dreaming.

THINGS THAT AFFECT CIRCADIAN RHYTHMS

- light and dark periods
- food and when it's eaten
- stress
- exercise or a lack of exercise
- social events
- temperature

SLEEP DRIVE

The sleep drive is our body's increasing need for sleep as the day goes on. That means we get tired as time passes. When we sleep, our sleep drive grows smaller. When we wake up after a good night of sleep, our sleep drive is at its weakest. We feel alert and ready to go!

The amount of light around a person affects sleep drive. When it gets darker, our bodies know it's getting closer to bedtime. A part of the brain sends out signals to the body. The body makes a **hormone** called melatonin. This is a chemical that helps us sleep.

When you don't get enough sleep, your sleep drive will kick in too early.

YAAAAAAAAWN

Circadian rhythms affect our sleep drive. For example, many people feel tired around 3 p.m. This "afternoon slump" can occur when you're at school or work. Getting a full night's rest can help. Other ways to avoid the afternoon slump include eating a healthy lunch, drinking water, and taking breaks to move or exercise. Learn more about the afternoon slump here: **www.webmd.com/balance/ss/slideshow-beat-afternoon-slump**

THE SLEEP CYCLE

A cycle is a set of steps or stages that happen more than once. The sleep cycle happens during a night of sleep, which can be broken down into 5 stages, shown here. “Drowsy” means sleepy. During light sleep, the body relaxes and breathing slows. “Moderate” means in the middle. During deep sleep, the body is at its most relaxed, allowing it to recover and grow. Turn the page to learn about REM sleep and dreaming.

SLEEP STAGES

If this sleep cycle is interrupted, or not allowed to finish, you're likely to feel drowsy the next day. You might even fall asleep in class!

DREAM ON!

Something strange happens during the fifth stage of the sleep cycle. After about 90 minutes, the brain gets very active, even though you're asleep. At the same time, the body becomes paralyzed for a short time. That means the body's **skeletal muscles** stop working!

REM means rapid eye movement. During this stage, the sleeper's eyes move wildly, as if watching things happening around them. This is when a sleeper is dreaming. This stage might only last a few minutes. As the sleep cycle repeats during the night, REM stages grow longer.

Dreams are often about people and things from our lives. They are shaped by the sleeper's thoughts, experiences, and beliefs. Dreaming allows the brain to make new connections and grow. Although dreams can seem **disjointed** and strange at times, they are our brain's attempt to process, or make sense of, recent experiences and new knowledge.

Scientists think our skeletal muscles become paralyzed during REM sleep so we don't act out our dreams.

Chapter 3

Sleep Problems

Cassie held the pillow tighter against her ears. It didn't help. She tossed the pillow across the room, hitting her older sister's head.

"Hey!" Angela yelled, sitting up in bed. Her bedside light came on. Cassie looked at her messy hair but was too tired to laugh. "I was sound asleep!"

"You're snoring worse than Dad!" Cassie said. "I need to get up early tomorrow for softball practice. I can't be tired!"

Angela responded by throwing the pillow back at Cassie. "I need to get up for work at 5:30! I can't be tired! It's bad enough that my snoring wakes me up, I don't need you waking me up too!"

The door to their room opened. Their dad stood in his pajamas, messy hair, yawning. "You guys need to quiet down, I have to get up early tomorrow!"

Snoring is one of the most common reasons for interrupted sleep—for the snorer and others around them!

I CAN'T SLEEP!

Many things can result in a bad night of sleep: barking dogs, beeping horns, thunder, physical pain, and more. We can usually find a way to deal with these things. Some health conditions can make it hard to sleep. There are ways to treat these conditions to help you get better sleep. But some sleep problems are more serious. These are called sleep disorders. Some are easier to treat than others.

Sleep apnea is a more serious form of snoring. It causes a person to stop breathing altogether until they wake up gasping for air. People with sleep apnea use a CPAP (continuous positive airway pressure) machine to breathe easy while sleeping. You can learn more about CPAP machines here: **my.clevelandclinic.org/health/treatments/22043-cpap-machine**

SNORING

Snoring is a common sleep problem. You might not even know that you snore unless someone tells you. For others, snoring becomes so bad it wakes the snorer up. It happens when the air flowing through your nose and mouth becomes blocked. Many things can cause this, such as a cold or allergies. Men snore more often than women. People tend to snore more or start snoring later in life. Other things that cause snoring include being overweight, drugs and alcohol, and a poor sleeping position.

WORRIED AND AWAKE

Have you ever been worried about an exam or group project at school? That can be a source of stress and anxiety for many students. Trying to sleep is hard when thoughts keep racing through your head, and when you can't seem to slow your heart rate and breathing. Depression can also cause sleeplessness.

If you think you have anxiety or depression, tell someone you trust. That could be a parent, a brother or sister, a friend, or a teacher. Don't suffer in silence—doctors will help you feel better! They will give you a check-up and ask some questions. Be as honest as you can. The doctor may give you a medication (drug) to take. Or they may tell you to stop another medication you are already taking. They may ask you to talk to a **therapist**.

Panic Attacks

People who struggle with stress, anxiety, and depression can have panic attacks that keep them awake at night. A panic attack is a sudden feeling of great fear, even though there's no danger.

Not being able to sleep, regardless of the reason, can result in chronic fatigue. That is a tiredness that happens frequently, perhaps every day.

WHAT KEEPS YOU AWAKE?

Stress, anxiety, and depression **manifest** as physical problems that make it hard to sleep. These in turn can result in drowsiness during the day.

- bruxism (grinding teeth)
- restless leg **syndrome**
- tight or sore muscles
- stomachache
- headache

COMMON SLEEP DISORDERS

Some adults develop restless leg syndrome (RLS) as they get older. This causes a person to want to move due to an uncomfortable feeling in the legs, especially at night. Moving the legs lessens the feeling, but it returns. Scientists aren't sure what causes RLS, but they know it can be affected by stress, caffeine, medications, genetics (it runs in the family), and other things. There's no cure for RLS, but there are ways to manage the symptoms, or signs. These usually include exercise and medication.

Scientists have identified more than 100 sleep disorders.

Here are more common sleep disorders.

- snoring and sleep apnea—See pages 22 and 23.
- insomnia—The general term for not being able to get to sleep or sleep through the night.
- narcolepsy—A problem in the brain that causes sudden sleepiness during the day.
- circadian rhythm disorders—Normal circadian rhythms can be disrupted by many things, including a changing work schedule and frequent travel (often called jet lag).

WHAT ARE PARASOMNIAS?

Parasomnias are unwanted activities that interrupt sleep. Parasomnias can be scary, but they're usually not harmful. Many things can cause parasomnias: missing or disrupted sleep, stress and anxiety, depression, disorders of the brain, and medications. They can also be genetic.

Common Parasomnias

- bedwetting
- sleep talking
- sleepwalking
- sleep eating

One of the more unusual parasomnias is called exploding head syndrome. When falling asleep, a person thinks they hear a very loud, sudden noise. It might be accompanied by a flash of light and muscle jerks. Scientist aren't sure what causes it.

MORE SERIOUS PARASOMNIAS

- REM sleep behavior disorder—Acting out dreams while asleep. This can include talking, shouting, laughing, punching, and kicking. It's more common in people with **neurodegenerative diseases**.
- sleep paralysis—An inability to move even though you just woke up. This can last for several minutes.
- nightmare disorder—Frequent vivid and scary dreams. Also called night terrors.

Chapter 4

TESTING AND TREATMENT

If you're having trouble sleeping, you may want to talk to your doctor. They will give you a check-up to make sure you are well. They will ask you questions about your daily life to get an idea of what might be causing your sleeplessness.

Doctors will start with simple suggestions to help you get more restful sleep. Exercise and diet (what we eat) can have an effect on how we sleep. Getting exercise every day prepares our minds and bodies for a good night of rest. Eating healthy foods and avoiding eating late can help as well.

The body makes a hormone called melatonin, which helps manage circadian rhythms. The body can make too much or too little melatonin, which can result in sleep disorders. Sometimes doctors will have you take melatonin pills to help you get to sleep, but it doesn't work for everyone.

Talking about your sleeping problems is the first step in getting better.

SEEING THE SOMNOLOGIST

Somnologists, or sleep specialists, are experts in diagnosing and treating sleep disorders. They may start by giving you a check-up. They will ask you questions. Depending on what they find, a somnologist may prescribe a medication. Or they may have you take part in a sleep study. They read the results of the study and help plan treatment. The treatment plan may include other doctors in different fields.

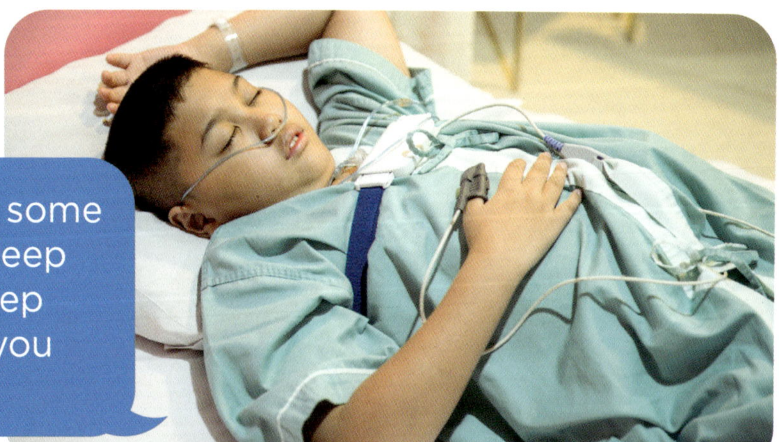

It's hard for some people to sleep during a sleep study. Can you tell why?

Sleep Study

Sleep studies are conducted by specialists called sleep technicians. During a sleep study, the patient will sleep in a medical building. Sleep technicians keep close watch on the patient's body systems, including heart rate, brain activity, and breathing. Much of this information is gathered using **sensors** placed on the patient's body.

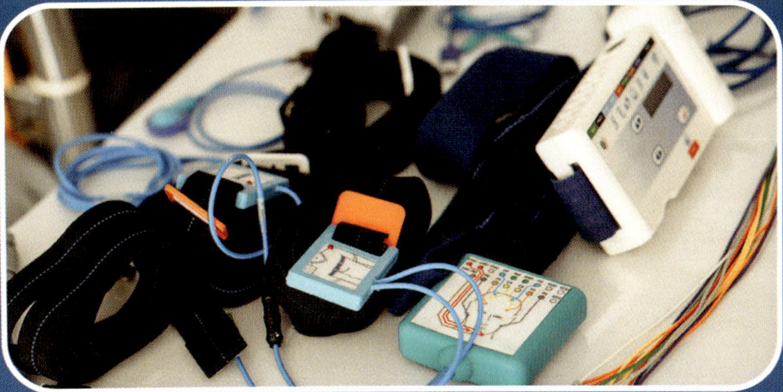

PREPARING FOR A SLEEP STUDY

- Follow your regular daily activities.
- Do not nap before the test.
- Do not drink coffee, soda, tea, or alcohol.
- Shower before the study.
- Pack an overnight bag.
- Let the doctor know if you take any medications.
- Let the doctor know if you have any allergies.

TREATING SLEEP DISORDERS

Treating a sleep disorder can be as easy as visiting your doctor once, but some disorders require ongoing care. The doctor may give you a medication. Or, they may tell you to stop using a medication that might be causing the disorder.

Doctors may ask you to change your sleep patterns if possible. Maybe you're tired because you're staying up too late! They may decide you need a CPAP machine to help you breathe at night. They may ask you to undergo **cognitive** behavioral therapy. This means talking to a trained therapist about your thoughts and emotions.

Light boxes like this one can be used in the home for easy light therapy treatments.

LIGHT THERAPY

Light therapy is a way to try to reset one's sleep-wake cycle. Several set times a day, a person sits in front of a "light box" that gives off light similar to sunlight. Sessions usually last 20 to 40 minutes. When used every day, light therapy can reset one's circadian rhythms, leading to a better night's rest.

Jeremy's Sleep Study

It was weird having wires taped all over me. There was an IV in my arm for medications, the nurse said. "It will help you relax." I didn't feel very relaxed yet!

The light slowly dimmed. I could hear a humming noise, somewhat like a waterfall. Dr. Navarro came in as the nurses were finishing. She smiled and gave my shoulder a friendly shake. "How you feeling, Jeremy? Sleepy?"

"Actually, yes." I yawned and Dr. Navarro laughed.

"Just lie back and relax, Jeremy. We're going to begin the test in a few minutes. When you wake up we'll have some stuff to talk about."

The doctor gave me another friendly shake and a smile before leaving me alone in the room. My eyes closed and I started to drift away . . .

Dr. Navarro's voice spoke softly from a speaker somewhere. "We're all ready, Jeremy. Give me a thumbs up."

I gave a thumbs up. My hand fell back to the bed. I fell asleep.

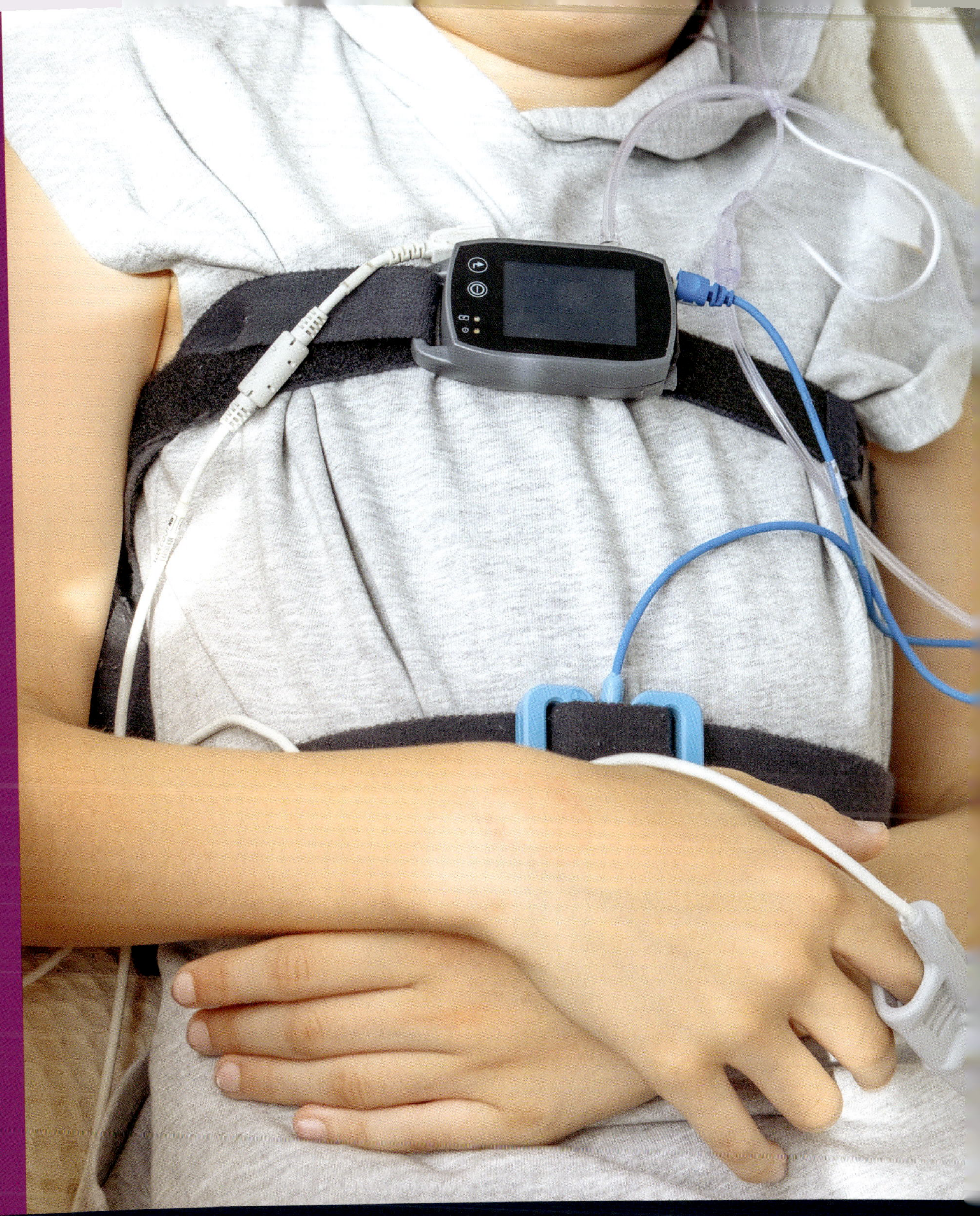

Chapter 5

LET'S TALK ABOUT HABITS

A habit is something that a person does regularly every day. Habits include things like mealtimes, exercise, and reading. It also includes things like biting our nails (a bad habit) and getting to sleep on time (a good habit). We are aware of many of our habits, but other habits are unconscious, meaning we don't know we're doing them. You might have a habit of cracking your knuckles even though it annoys people around you.

Our daily habits, both good and bad, have a large effect on how well we sleep. That's because our habits can affect our circadian rhythms. Some habits promote a healthy sleep schedule while others can disrupt it.

One habit that can be bad for teens is spending too much time in the room where they sleep. There's nothing wrong with hanging out in your room alone. But doing it too often can result in a disrupted sleep schedule. It will also eat into time you could spend exercising and hanging out with friends and family.

THE GOOD AND THE BAD

Some habits are good because they help keep our circadian rhythms in healthy order. Some habits are bad because they interrupt circadian rhythms.

Regular exercise helps your body use up its energy, and allows you to sleep well. Meditating during the day helps reduce stress that may keep you awake at night.

GOOD HABITS

- exercising regularly
- eating healthy foods on a regular schedule
- reading before going to sleep
- limiting drinks before bed so you don't wake up to use the bathroom
- learning healthy ways to manage stress
- meditating, or taking 10 to 20 minutes to clear your mind and focus on how the body feels

BAD HABITS

- drinking too much caffeine
- eating too much close to bedtime
- doing drugs not okayed by a doctor
- drinking alcohol
- smoking/vaping
- staying up late
- napping during the day
- staring at computer or phone screens before bed

BEING MINDFUL

Mindfulness is somewhat like meditation. It's the practice of using the five senses to be "fully present" in an activity. This means the mind is fully focused on where it is and what it's doing without being distracted by other thoughts. Sometimes our minds drift away. Instead of allowing our thoughts to complicate an issue, mindfulness keeps your brain focused.

Mindfulness practices are incredibly helpful for many reasons. They are used as a therapy tool to help people overcome things like depression and anxiety. It can also be used to help keep our circadian rhythms in check and make sure you are relaxed and ready for sleep.

It can be tough living with a sleep disorder. But now you know that there's no reason to live with one.

You can learn a lot more about mindfulness and mindfulness practices here:

- **www.mindfulnessforteens.com**
- **anxiety-gone.com/mindfulness-activities-for-teens**

Well Rested!

The bell rang to end third period, math class was over. Tia had already placed her notebook in her backpack. She hummed as she walked to the door.

"Tia, can I talk to you real quick?" said Mr. Robelard.

"Sure!" she said with a smile. "What's up?"

He handed her a piece of paper. It was the quiz the class had taken on Monday. "100%" was written at the top in green ink.

"Great work, Tia! That was a tough one too. You haven't fallen asleep in class for several weeks, and you're grade is going back up. Seems like you've made some good changes."

Tia nodded. "I was having a hard time sleeping at night. My parents took me to a doctor, and he sent me to a sleep specialist." She laughed. " I had no idea I was sleeping all wrong! I've been dealing with a lot of stress at home, but the specialist helped me cope with my feelings better. I'm sleeping much better now!"

GLOSSARY

allergy: An abnormal reaction (sneezing, itching, or rashes) to substances, situations, or physical states that do not have such a strong effect on most people.

anxiety: Fear or nervousness about what might happen.

automatic: Happening without thought, or happening immediately.

chemical: Matter that can be mixed with other matter to cause changes.

cognitive: Relating to brain activities.

concentrate: To focus, or direct, one's attention.

depression: A mood disorder marked by sadness, despair, and loneliness usually accompanied by social withdrawal, inactivity, and loss of a sense of one's own worth.

disjointed: Not clear or orderly.

disorder: A physical or mental condition.

hormone: A natural substance produced in the body that controls the way the body develops.

manifest: To show plainly.

neurodegenerative disease: One of many illnesses that cause the nervous system (brain, spinal column, and nerves) to break down over time.

schedule: A list of times when certain events will or should happen.

sensor: A device that detects something and sends information to something else.

skeletal muscle: The type of muscle that connects to bones and allows us to move our body.

stress: Something that causes strong feelings of worry.

syndrome: A group of symptoms, or signs, that occur together and characterize a particular illness or condition.

therapist: One trained in methods of treatment and rehabilitation other than the use of drugs or surgery.

INDEX